D1566772

Miranda Lambert

ABDO
Publishing Company

Big Buddy BOOKS
Buddy Bios

by **Sarah Tieck**

VISIT US AT
www.abdopublishing.com

Published by ABDO Publishing Company, 8000 West 78th Street, Edina, Minnesota 55439.

Printed in the United States of America, North Mankato, Minnesota.
062011
092011

 PRINTED ON RECYCLED PAPER

Coordinating Series Editor: Rochelle Baltzer
Contributing Editors: Megan M. Gunderson, BreAnn Rumsch, Marcia Zappa
Graphic Design: Maria Hosley
Cover Photograph: *AP Photo*: Dan Steinberg.
Interior Photographs/Illustrations: *AP Photo*: Evan Agostini (p. 17), Gregg DeGuire/PictureGroup via AP IMAGES
    (p. 9), Kristian Dowling/PictureGroup via AP IMAGES (p. 18), Mike Fuentes (p. 6), Scott Gries/PictureGroup
    via AP IMAGES (p. 5), Curtis Hilbun (pp. 12, 23), Julie Jacobson (p. 27), Peter Kramer (p. 22), NBC/NBC
    NewsWire via AP Images (p. 20), Chris Pizzello (p. 29), Matt Sayles (p. 19), Tim Sharp (p. 13), Dan Steinberg
    (p. 17), Mark J. Terrill (p. 15); *Getty Images*: Rick Diamond/Getty Images for CMT (p. 27), Rick Diamond/
    Getty Images for Front Porch Farms (p. 27), Christopher Polk/ACMA 2011/Getty Images for ACM (p. 24), John
    Russell/WireImage (p. 11).

Library of Congress Cataloging-in-Publication Data

Tieck, Sarah, 1976-
  Miranda Lambert : country music star / Sarah Tieck.
    p. cm. -- (Big buddy biographies)
  ISBN 978-1-61783-018-1
  1. Lambert, Miranda, 1983---Juvenile literature. 2. Country musicians--United States--Biography--Juvenile
literature. I. Title.
  ML3930.L145T54 2012
  782.421642092--dc23
  [B]
                                2011018226

Miranda
Lambert

Contents

Singing Star

Miranda Lambert is a country singer and songwriter. She has won awards for her hit albums and songs.

Miranda is well known. She has appeared on magazine covers. And, she has been **interviewed** on popular television shows.

When Miranda was very young, her father worked as a police officer. Later, her parents both became private investigators. They helped solve crimes!

6

Family Ties

Miranda Leigh Lambert was born in Longview, Texas, on November 10, 1983. Miranda's parents are Rick and Bev Lambert. Her younger brother is named Luke.

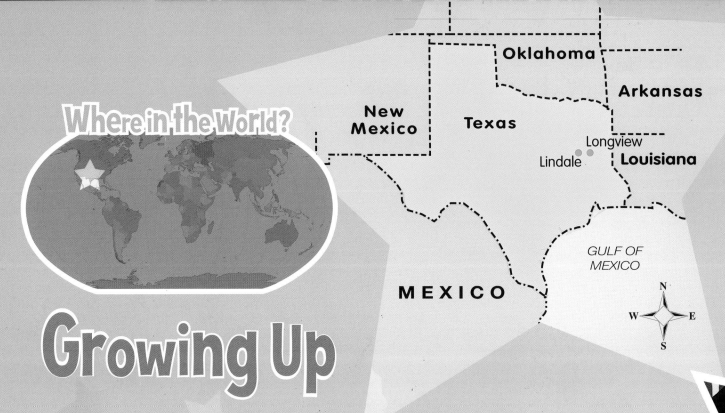

Growing Up

When Miranda was about six, her life changed. Her parents lost their business. So, her family moved to her uncle's farm.

Soon, Miranda's parents started working again. And, they got their own farm. They grew food in their garden. They canned pickles and made bread. They also ate hogs and rabbits they raised.

Miranda grew up in the small town of Lindale, Texas. She spent a lot of time with her brother, Luke (*left*). They are still close.

Did you know...

Young Miranda enjoyed music. She would listen to her dad play songs by famous country singer Merle Haggard. Miranda was very excited when she got to meet Merle in 2005!

Starting Out

Miranda wanted to become a country singer. Her family supported her dream. As a teenager, Miranda **performed** in places close to her home.

In 2003, Miranda took part in *Nashville Star*. This was a singing **competition** on television. She won third place! Because of the show, people began noticing her talent.

Miranda didn't want to win *Nashville Star*. She didn't think she was ready to make a record. But, competing helped improve her singing skills.

In 2005, Miranda performed for a Country Music Television special with Blake Shelton. They became close friends.

First Album

Soon, Miranda got a record deal. In 2005, she released an album called *Kerosene*. People liked her bold, wild style.

Kerosene became popular on country music charts. In 2006, Miranda was nominated for a Grammy Award. Even though she didn't win the award, this was a big honor.

Miranda wrote many of the songs on *Kerosene*. She and her dad wrote "Greyhound Bound for Nowhere" together.

Building a Career

Miranda's popularity continued to grow. Soon, Miranda was **interviewed** for magazines and television shows.

In 2007, Miranda **released** another album, *Crazy Ex-Girlfriend*. This album had several hit songs. In 2008, Miranda won an Academy of Country Music (ACM) award for her work.

Miranda won the ACM award for Album of the Year!

15

Talented Singer

In 2009, Miranda **released** her third major album. It is called *Revolution*. This album was a hit! In 2010, Miranda was **nominated** for six ACM awards. She won three of them! And, she won three awards from the Country Music Association (CMA).

At both the ACM (*left*) and CMA (*right*) awards, Miranda received special trophies to honor her work.

Miranda's music was **nominated** for five awards at the 2011 **Grammys**. One nomination was for Best Female Country Vocal **Performance** for the song "The House That Built Me." She won!

Miranda had been nominated for Grammys before. But 2011 was the first time she won.

At the 2011 Grammys, Miranda sang "The House That Built Me."

Miranda enjoys singing live for her fans.

A Singer's Life

Miranda works hard on her music. She writes many of her own songs. After much practice, she records them. Miranda spends many hours working on her albums in a **studio**.

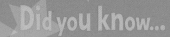
After releasing an album, Miranda often goes on tour. She travels and performs live concerts. When Miranda is not recording or performing, she attends events and meets fans. Her fans are often very excited to see her!

In 2009, Miranda toured with country singer Kenny Chesney.

Miranda toured with Blake Shelton in 2008. She sang songs from her albums.

Miranda and Blake were friends before they fell in love.

Did you know...

Miranda and Blake like to help others. They have performed in concerts to raise money for animal shelters.

Off the Stage

In Miranda's free time, she likes to be at home. She also likes to spend time with friends and family. On May 14, 2011, she married country singer Blake Shelton.

Farm Girl

Miranda's home is a farm in Oklahoma. She owns 700 acres (283 ha) of land. When she isn't **performing**, she likes to wear jeans and work on the farm.

Miranda has many animals at her farm. She has adopted seven dogs. And, Blake gave her a miniature horse!

Miranda and Blake had a farm party to honor their plans to get married.

One of Miranda's dogs is a chihuahua named Cher!

Blake also enjoys farming. He has his own farm near Miranda's.

Buzz

Today, Miranda's fame continues to grow. She keeps busy writing and singing new songs. In 2011, Miranda began working on a new album.

Fans are excited to see what's next for Miranda Lambert. Many believe she has a bright **future**!

MGM GRA
LAS VEG

ACADEMY
of COUNTRY MUSIC
AWARDS

MGM GR
LAS VE

29

Snapshot

☆ **Name**: Miranda Leigh Lambert

☆ **Birthday**: November 10, 1983

☆ **Birthplace**: Longview, Texas

☆ **Albums**: *Kerosene, Crazy Ex-Girlfriend, Revolution*

Important Words

chart a list that shows which music has sold the most during a period of time.

competition (kahm-puh-TIH-shuhn) a contest between two or more persons or groups. To compete is to take part in a competition.

future (FYOO-chuhr) a time that has not yet occurred.

Grammy Award any of the awards given each year by the National Academy of Recording Arts and Sciences. Grammy Awards honor the year's best accomplishments in music.

interview to ask someone a series of questions.

nominate to name as a possible winner.

perform to do something in front of an audience. A performance is the act of doing something, such as singing or acting, in front of an audience.

release to make available to the public.

studio a place where music is recorded.

Web Sites

To learn more about Miranda Lambert, visit ABDO Publishing Company online. Web sites about Miranda Lambert are featured on our Book Links page. These links are routinely monitored and updated to provide the most current information available.

www.abdopublishing.com

Index